W9-ADO-298

A Forest Year

A Forest Year

CAROL · LERNER

WILLIAM MORROW AND COMPANY, INC.
NEW YORK

For Joshua, linked in my memory to the Leaning Beech

The author thanks Charles Nelson, director of the Sarett Nature Center in
Benton Harbor, Michigan, for his cheerful review of the text.

Copyright © 1987 by Carol Lerner
All rights reserved.
No part of this book may be reproduced
or utilized in any form or by any means,
electronic or mechanical, including photocopying,
recording or by any information storage and retrieval system,
without permission in writing from the Publisher.
Inquiries should be addressed to
William Morrow and Company, Inc.,
105 Madison Avenue, New York, NY 10016.
Printed in Hong Kong.
1 2 3 4 5 6 7 8 9 10
Library of Congress Cataloging-in-Publication Data
Lerner, Carol.
A forest year.
Summary: Describes how seasonal changes in a forest
affect the plants and animals that live there.
1. Forest ecology—Juvenile literature.   2. Seasons—Juvenile literature.
[1. Forest ecology.   2. Seasons.   3. Ecology]   I. Title.
QH541.5.F6L44   1987   574.5'2642   86-9741
ISBN 0-688-06413-2
ISBN 0-688-06414-0 (lib. bdg.)

Most forests of the eastern half of the United States are filled with broad-leaved trees that grow new leaves each spring and drop them before winter comes. As the leaves fall, the sunny comfort of summer slowly gives way to short days and freezing temperatures. These changes shape the life of every plant and animal in the woodlands.

This book looks at some common forest plants and animals in each season to see how they live through the year.

1995 BTT 12⁹⁵

WINTER—MAMMALS

Animals that fly can get away from cold weather by travel-ing great distances. Bats are the only flying mammals; some go south for the winter, and others go only as far as a cave or some other protected place. All the other woodland mam-mals must find shelter closer to home. Most of them crawl into nests and sleep a lot during the coldest weeks of the year. A very few go into hibernation as their bodies undergo a great change: Their temperatures drop, their heartbeats and breathing become very slow, and for months they do not eat or drink. Other animals are active all winter long.

The fluffy snow is like a blanket, and the soil beneath it may be fifty degrees warmer than the winter air. Some mammals live in underground homes all year. This habit protects them from the freezing temperatures of winter.

In summer WOODCHUCKS live in underground holes in open fields and grasslands, but they often move to the forest to make winter dens. They are true hibernators.

SHREWS live in underground homes, too. They tunnel through the ground and under the snow in their endless search for something to eat. Their bodies use up food so quickly that a shrew would die if it stopped eating for seven or eight hours. Their usual food is small animals, such as insects and worms, but in winter they also eat roots, nuts, and other plant food.

WHITE-FOOTED MICE climb easily and often have nests up in trees. They find tree holes or old woodpecker nests and make soft beds of leaves inside. On the coldest days the mice stay in their nests, but usually they go out to eat from stored piles of nuts and seeds and to look for more food.

DEER may move from their summer territory to another wooded area where there is more winter food. They rest in any hidden spot that gives shelter from the wind and snow. They feed mostly at night on twigs and barks.

WINTER-BIRDS

Even with layers of down feathers, birds need a lot of food to keep them warm when the air is cold. Many woodland birds move to the south long before the chill of winter, but some stay all year around. Still other birds, such as kinglets and brown creepers, fly down from the North Woods of Canada and the northernmost parts of the United States; they come to spend the winter where the weather is less cold. Each day the birds move through the woods in a busy search for food. At night they find shelter where they can: in tree holes or hidden in the branches of evergreen trees.

Birds often band together in winter to make up small feeding groups. Sometimes all birds in the group are of one kind. CARDINALS gather into a loose flock of both males and females and often feed on the ground. Most of their winter food comes from plants. They search for the seeds of tulip trees, dogwoods, grapes, and other forest plants.

Other groups have several different kinds of birds, all feeding together. These birds are looking for insects, but each hunts in a way that is a little different from the others: CHICKADEES hang from twigs, WOODPECKERS drill into trees, NUTHATCHES move up and down tree trunks, and CREEPERS, with their long, curved bills, get into places under the bark where other birds cannot reach.

A ruffed grouse made the TRACKS on the snow. In the fall a feathery comb grows on the grouse's feet, making them like snowshoes. The grouse feeds on the ground and in tree branches on buds, dried-up berries, and evergreen needles. Sometimes it digs into the snow for a warm sleeping place.

The lumps under the evergreen tree tell that an owl has rested in this tree after a nighttime hunt for food. After the owl has fed, it throws up lumpy PELLETS. They contain the bones and other tough parts of its prey—usually mice, sometimes a small bird.

grouse
foot

WINTER—REPTILES AND AMPHIBIANS

All reptiles and amphibians are "cold-blooded"—that is, their bodies are never much warmer than the temperature of whatever surrounds them. Cold weather slows down the workings of their bodies, and freezing can kill them. Before winter comes, they search out places where they will have some protection from the cold, and most of them go into hibernation. Many frogs, salamanders, and turtles spend winter in water, below the frozen layer of ice or in the mud below. But some of them, along with snakes and lizards, stay on land through the cold months.

BOX TURTLES are the only turtles in the forest that live their whole lives on land. In winter they find soft ground and dig down a few inches to resting places. As the temperature of the soil drops, the animals dig in a little deeper. By the end of the winter they may be two feet down in the earth.

Rocky caves are favorite shelters for hibernating snakes, but they also use rotting logs or holes in the ground made by other animals. Some kinds of snakes, such as RING-NECKED SNAKES, may twist together to form a living ball. Snakes that hibernate in this way lose less heat and moisture over the winter.

Amphibians, such as salamanders and frogs, easily lose body water through their thin skins. The species that spend the winter on land and aboveground face a double danger : Their bodies may freeze, or else they may lose too much body moisture and dry up. They need shelters that are damp as well as protected from the cold. SPOTTED SALAMANDERS and the "masked" WOOD FROG may crawl under rotting logs or layers of old leaves on the forest floor to hibernate.

WINTER−INSECTS

A handful of insects make long-distance journeys to warmer places for the winter, just as birds do. The monarch butterfly is the best known of these. But most insects move only for short distances when winter comes: They go deeper into logs or trees, to the bottom of dead plant stems, into the layer of dead leaves on the ground, or down into the earth. As with reptiles and amphibians, insect bodies slow down in the cold. Almost all of them enter a resting period when winter comes. An insect starts life as an egg and changes its shape several times as it grows to an adult. Some kinds live through the cold months in the form of eggs, some as adults, and some in the in-between stages as a larva, pupa, or nymph.

OYSTER-SHELL SCALE INSECTS pass the winter as eggs under the "scale," that is the dead body of their mother. In late summer or fall, each female lays up to one hundred eggs on a twig and dies soon afterward. Most kinds of adult scale insects are very small; eight of these scales in a row measure one inch.

WOOLLY BEAR CATERPILLARS (the larval stage of an Isabella moth) and adult MOURNING CLOAK BUTTERFLIES may spend the winter under loose bark. On warm days they sometimes wake and come out from their shelter.

All the members of a WHITE-FACED HORNET nest die in the fall except the adult queens. Each queen goes off alone, chews out a hole in a rotting log, and spends the winter there.

In winter adult LADYBIRD BEETLES (ladybugs) cluster in groups of hundreds. They may gather under the dead leaves on the forest floor.

MAY BEETLES (also called June bugs) pass most of their lives underground and may spend the winter as an adult or as a larva. They go deep in the earth, where the ground does not freeze.

Tiny SPRINGTAILS (snow fleas) are one of the few insects that are active in winter. Swarms of them appear on mild days, hopping on the snow. They spend the winter as adults, feeding on soft and decaying plant matter on the ground.

oyster-shell scales

springtail

WINTER—PLANTS

When freezing weather comes, water in the soil turns to ice and cannot be used by plant roots. Forest plants meet the problems of frozen water and freezing air in different ways. Some of the small plants with soft stems die completely at the end of the growing season. These plants, called annuals, *continue life only in the seeds they have left behind. Other soft-stemmed plants dry up aboveground but stay alive in underground parts (bulbs, corms, rhizomes, and tubers) down in the earth. The woody plants—trees and bushes— have parts both above and below ground that stay alive all winter. Most of them have bare branches now; they have dropped the leaves that give off water during the growing season. Their branches and trunks are wrapped with bark that protects them and keeps them from drying up.*

The summer has left behind a harvest of SEEDS in berries and acorns, pods, nuts, and other fruits. Many will feed the forest animals. A few will stay on the ground and start new plants when warm weather comes again.

Most of the small forest plants live for many years, even though the parts aboveground die down before winter. UNDERGROUND PARTS hold extra food made by the plant during the past year's growing season. This will feed the young stems, leaves, and flowers that shoot up next spring.

The leaves and flowers of next spring's trees and bushes are already formed—in miniature. They are covered and kept moist by tight bud scales. Winter buds on each kind of plant have their own special shape and arrangement: OAK BUDS grow in clusters, and BEECH BUDS are long and pointed.

EVERGREEN PLANTS have leaves on their branches all winter, but many evergreens have leaves in the shape of needles or scales. These lose less water than broad, flat leaves. They are smaller and often have a hard, waxy surface that holds in moisture. They have fewer of the "breathing pores" that give off water from plants.

oak buds

beech buds

SPRING—MAMMALS

As the days become warmer, the hibernators and deep sleepers leave their winter dens. They wake up hungry, and their first business is to find food. But some of the animals that were up and about all winter are already busy taking care of their babies, born in late winter. Before the spring is over, most of the adult female mammals in the forest will be raising new families. Many of the plant eaters will have two or more litters before winter comes again; mammals that live only on meat give birth just once each year.

WOODLAND VOLES (or pine voles) spend most of their time in tunnels a few inches under the ground. Their babies are born in nests in the ground or under stones or logs. They have three or four litters a year. The young voles grow quickly and are ready to find their own food after two or three weeks.

A female RABBIT may give birth four or more times between early spring and fall, and usually four or five babies are born in each litter. After two weeks the young rabbits begin to leave the nest and to feed on grass and other plant foods.

OPOSSUMS feed on many kinds of food: insects, dead animals, eggs, and all sorts of fruits and berries. Young opossums are smaller than a honeybee at birth. For the first two months of their lives their eyes are closed, and they never leave their mother's furry pouch. She carries them around wherever she goes. Even after they grow out of the pouch, they hold on to her back and ride along with her for another month or more. After the young have become independent, the mother may have a second litter of babies before summer is over.

Unlike most forest animals, both parents of young FOXES care for the babies. The young, usually three to six, are born during the spring in a den that may be underground or in a hollow log. At first the pups are blind and helpless. By three months of age they are learning to hunt for rabbits and mice. They are ready to leave their parents by fall.

Slowly at first and then with a rush, birds from the south stream into the spring woodlands. Most of the travelers stop only long enough to rest and feed and then continue north or else scatter to other places. Those that stay, together with the year-round birds of this woodland, are soon busy with the serious business of the season. The males search out nesting places that are close to a good supply of food. They fill the woods with song as they lay claim to their chosen spaces and call for females. Then the pairs begin to mate, nest, and raise the young.

Many forest birds, both those that stay only during the warmer weather and a large number of the year-round residents, use tree holes for nests. HAIRY WOODPECKERS often nest in live trees; the smaller DOWNY WOODPECKERS look for dead ones. Woodpeckers and BLACK-CAPPED CHICKADEES peck out their own nests. Some other birds depend on finding ready-made holes.

Male birds chase other males of their own kind away from their territory, but birds of different species may live and nest very close to one another without fighting. Sometimes these close neighbors even belong to the same bird group. Ovenbirds, hooded warblers, and cerulean warblers all are wood warblers. All three may nest in the shade of the same tree, but each pair lives in a different layer of the woodland. OVENBIRDS build covered nests on the ground. HOODED WARBLERS make their neat cups a few feet above the ground in low vines or bushes. The CERULEANS use the high branches of tall trees.

cerulean warbler

Pease Public Library
Plymouth, NH 03264-1414

SPRING—REPTILES AND AMPHIBIANS

The winter ice has melted now, and the water and the earth are warming slowly. After lying cold and quiet all winter long, in the ground or on the pond bottom, the reptiles and amphibians are warming, too. When their temperatures become high enough, they begin to come out from their resting places. Most of them will be looking for mates soon. Male frogs and toads call out to attract the attention of the females. From early spring their cries fill the night air.

Toads and frogs gather at woodland ponds, streams, and puddles in the spring. Even the little SPRING PEEPER, which spends its adult life on land, heads for water, where it will mate and deposit its eggs. Like all amphibians, frogs and toads lay eggs that are covered with jelly but have no outer shells to protect them. In the water the eggs are safe from drying out.

Some kinds of salamanders mate in the fall and produce eggs as soon as they come out of hibernation. The SLIMY SALAMANDER is one of the few salamanders that lay eggs on land. The female lays them in earliest spring in moist, protected places—under wet, rotting logs or in damp moss. Unlike other amphibians, the salamanders that lay on land often stay to look after the eggs until they hatch.

WOOD TURTLES spend most of their lives on land, but in the spring they are often near water. Like frogs, these turtles call out for a mate, making a sound like a whistling teakettle. When she lays her eggs in the summer, the female will bury them in a hole in the ground and leave them to be hatched by the heat of the sun. All reptile eggs are covered by tough shells and are laid on land.

Like most other snakes, the HOGNOSE SNAKE (or puff adder) mates soon after it has come out in spring, before the group that has shared the hibernating place scatters. In summer the female will lay her eggs—usually fifteen to twenty —and leave them under a log or flat stone.

SPRING—INSECTS

The insects begin to stir and crawl from their winter hiding places. Everywhere in the forest, from the treetops to the soil underfoot, thousands of different kinds of insects begin to move and change. Many that lived through the cold months as eggs will hatch out now as some kind of larva or nymph. Other insects will come out of cocoons or another sort of pupa case and become adults as the new season begins. Insect changes are tied to the lives of the plants and other animals in the spring forest: As the plant buds open and more and more animals become active, the insects that feed on each of these appear, too.

Most wildflowers and many of the trees and bushes need the help of insects to spread the pollen from flower to flower. Many kinds of bees and wasps, butterflies and moths, beetles and flies come to these plants to feed on pollen and sweet nectar. Pollen dust sticks to their bodies and is carried to the next flower they visit. Queen BUMBLEBEES live through the winter and come out when the first flowers bloom. They collect pollen in special honey baskets on their back legs.

SPRING AZURES are one of the first butterflies to change from pupa to adult in the spring. They sometimes appear in the woods even before all of the snow has melted from the ground.

TENT CATERPILLARS hatch from an egg cluster laid on the twig of a wild cherry tree. They live together in a silky tent that they spin in the fork of a branch. The caterpillars leave the tent to feed on buds and leaves.

Large ground beetles called CATERPILLAR HUNTERS come out at night to feed on tent caterpillars and other insects that eat plants. Sometimes the beetles climb into trees to find their prey. During the day they hide from sight.

tent caterpillar
nest

SPRING—PLANTS

Forest plants explode in new growth. One by one, and in an order that is the same each year, each different kind of plant comes into flower. Every new day in spring brings a few extra minutes of daylight; each species of plant begins to flower only after its own special period of "day length" has been reached. The forest floor comes to life first, as spring wildflowers push through the carpet of dead leaves. They bloom quickly. By the time the leaves on the treetops put the forest floor in shadow, most forest wildflowers have finished their flowering for the year.

TROUT LILY is one of the little woodland wildflowers that shoot up, flower, and make fruits and seeds quickly—all within a few weeks' time. Then the parts of the plant that grow aboveground dry up and disappear. In this short time the plant has also made a supply of extra food and sent it underground for storage. This food keeps the plant alive all through the rest of the year, when there are no green leaves aboveground, and supplies the energy that will send up new stems and flowers next spring.

As soon as its buds begin to open in the spring, a tree starts growing inside its trunk and all its branches. A thin layer called the *cambium,* which lines a tree's bark like an inside skin, begins to make new cells. The new cells on the inside of the cambium layer will become part of the *sapwood* that brings water, along with minerals dissolved in it, from the ground up to the leaves. The new cells on the outside of the cambium layer become the *phloem.* This layer carries food made by the leaves to all the other parts of the tree.

Plants make seeds after pollen from the male flower parts has reached the female parts. The TULIP TREE depends on insects to spread the pollen. The HICKORY and most of the other forest trees have very small flowers whose pollen is spread by the wind.

female flowers   male flowers

hickory

tulip tree

bark

phloem

cambium

sapwood

SUMMER—MAMMALS

Now the whole forest is green and growing, and there is plenty of food for the animals that feed on plants. As young rabbits and chipmunks and mice leave their mothers and begin to take care of themselves, more and more mammals are moving through the forest. This makes summer an easier time for the hunting animals as well. Darkness gives some protection from enemies, so most of the plant eaters come out to feed when the sun is going down. That is when the hunters come out, too.

BATS fly at night, catching insects in the air. As they fly, bats make a noise so high in pitch that a human ear cannot hear it. The bats catch food and find their way in the dark by following the echo of this sound as it bounces back off trees, flying insects, and other objects.

FLYING SQUIRRELS feed on nuts, seeds, and other parts of plants. Animal food—mostly insects—is a smaller part of their diet. They glide through the night air by jumping from trees. When their legs are spread, flaps of skin on each side of the bodies become furry sails. The thin, flat tails help them to steer. Their large eyes can see well in the dark.

In the evening, RACCOON mothers lead their young down from their dens in hollow trees. Together they go looking for something to eat. Raccoons like every kind of food: fruits and vegetables, seeds, insects, meat, bird eggs.

TREE SQUIRRELS (gray, red, and fox squirrels) usually are out during the day. At night they sleep in nests up in a tree. Chipmunks and tree squirrels are the only common forest mammals that are most active in broad daylight.

Most songbirds become quiet when nesting starts. In two weeks or so, when the eggs hatch, the hardest work of the parents begins. Their young are born blind and helpless and need large amounts of food. In early summer almost the whole adult bird community is busy caring for their newly hatched babies. Usually both parents take part—hunting for food and stuffing it down the open mouths of the young. Even among seed-eating birds, most food given to the young is animal food—mainly insects and spiders. Different kinds of birds use different parts of the forest for their hunting grounds: Some search the forest floor; others use tree trunks or treetops.

Vireos are small songbirds that search the trees and bushes for insects. Their main food is caterpillars and moths, bugs and beetles, which they pick up from leaves and twigs. YELLOW-THROATED VIREOS and RED-EYED VIREOS may be nesting in the same forest and hunting for the same insects. They stay out of each other's way because they feed at different heights from the ground: Yellow-throateds stay in the treetops most of the time, while red-eyes usually search in the middle and lower branches.

REDSTART WARBLERS, like vireos, eat insects from the twigs and branches of trees, but the way they feed is different. Redstarts circle up and down through the branches, often catching flying insects in midair. Their open mouths make good insect traps; they are wide at the bottom and surrounded by stiff bristles.

The RUFFED GROUSE is one of the rare forest-nesting birds whose young come out of the eggs with full coats of soft feathers and with open eyes. As soon as the young chicks dry off, they follow their mother from the nest and wander through the woods, looking for insects on the ground. At night, and when it is cold or raining, the mother protects them under her wings. The chicks stay with their mother through the summer, but they never return to the nest.

yellow-throated
vireo

redstart
warbler

red-eyed
vireo

SUMMER—REPTILES AND AMPHIBIANS

The frogs and toads of the forest left their eggs behind in the water when they mated in spring, but some of the other amphibians and the reptiles do not lay eggs or give birth until summer. When the young hatch or are born and begin to search for food, there is plenty to eat in the summer woods. But for some of these animals, summer weather can also be dangerous: Because their body temperatures are close to the temperatures of the air or water around them, they may overheat on sunny days. Those in water can cool off by swimming to the bottom of the pond or burying themselves in the mud below. The land dwellers solve the problem by resting in cool places during the warmest time of day and feeding at night or when the sun is low in the sky.

The FIVE-LINED SKINK is a small lizard with a long tail. The female makes a nest hole under a log or a flat rock and lays her eggs there. She stays with them for four to seven weeks, her body looped around the eggs, until they hatch. During this time she will leave the nest only for short periods to feed or to warm her body in the sunshine.

In the summer heat COMMON TOADS dig shallow holes in the cool earth and stay there during the warmest hours. In the cool of evening they come out to hunt for flies, mosquitoes, and other insects.

Red-spotted newts are salamanders that live in water, but before they become adults, they spend two or three years on land. At this earlier stage the newts are called RED EFTS. They often crawl about the forest floor in broad daylight, especially after rainstorms, looking for insects to eat.

BLACK SNAKES (or black racers) are slim animals, three or four feet in length. They eat all kinds of small animals—mice, snakes and lizards, frogs and toads, birds and their eggs—capturing them by looping their bodies around the victim. Like many other cold-blooded animals, they control their body heat by moving to different parts of the woods as the temperature changes. When it is too cool, they lie in the sun to warm up ; when it is too hot, they crawl into the shade.

SUMMER—INSECTS

Nothing growing in the forest is safe from an insect that feeds on it. Some insects eat leaves, some drink plant juices, and others chew into tree trunks and branches. By late summer many leaves in the forest are ragged and spotted, showing signs of insect damage. But birds and hunting insects are always moving through the leaves and branches, too, and they kill and eat many of the plant-feeding insects.

CICADAS are the largest sap-sucking insects of the forest. The nymphs live underground and feed on sap in tree roots. They stay there from two to seventeen years, depending on the species, and come up only when they are ready to change to adults. Adult males make loud, buzzing noises from the trees, calling for mates.

SUGAR-MAPLE BORERS are striped black beetles that lay eggs in the bark of maple trees. After they have hatched, the larvae enter the layer under the bark and eat their way all around the tree's trunk.

More kinds of insects feed on leaves than on any other part of a tree. Those that tunnel between the tough top and bottom layers of a leaf while eating the juicy inside parts are called LEAF MINERS. The larvae of many different kinds of insects feed in this way.

APHIDS (plant lice) are small, soft insects with pear-shaped bodies. To feed, they push their mouth parts into a plant and suck its juices. The larvae of LACEWINGS are called *aphid lions*. As soon as they hatch, lacewings begin to kill aphids and other small insects by sucking out their blood. Adults feed in the same way.

Galls grow where some insect has cut into a plant, either to feed or to lay an egg there. About 1,500 kinds of gall-making insects live in North America, and each kind causes a different sort of gall to form. Big, round OAK APPLE GALLS grow on oak leaves after a small wasp has laid her egg on the stem or vein. After hatching, the young insect feeds and grows inside the gall.

oak apple gall

leaf miner

lacewing larva
with aphid

SUMMER—PLANTS

The summer forest is one great food factory. All through the long, sun-filled days every green leaf is making food that nourishes the living plants, feeds their growth, and packs away energy for the needs of the future. The forest plants growing beneath the tall trees are in shadow for most of the summer. Short bursts of sunshine, breaking through the leafy umbrella, give the understory plants enough light to make food for their needs.

A fully grown forest of broad-leaved trees has layers of plant life at different heights. The bottom one is the small plants on the ground—wildflowers, ferns, grasses—and the top layer is made up of the leafy branches of the large forest trees. In between are a layer of bushes and another of smaller trees. Some of the small trees are kinds that never grow very big, and others are younger trees that will reach the highest layer when they are older.

Green leaves get their color from *chlorophyll*, bits of green matter that fill their inner layers. Chlorophyll makes food. The raw materials are water, brought up from the roots through leaf veins, and gases that enter through tiny holes on the underside of the leaf. With the energy in sunlight supplying the power, chlorophyll changes parts of these materials into sugar. The sugar, dissolved in water, flows back into the plant through the veins to feed all its living parts.

The TALL BELLFLOWER is one of the few plants that flower in the summer woods. Most of the summer-blooming wildflowers of the forest grow on the edges or in openings, where more sunshine reaches them.

Ferns have no flowers or seeds; instead, they produce spores. In CHRISTMAS FERN and most other species, small bumps called *sori* grow on the undersides of some of the fern's leaves in summer. These are little cases holding great numbers of tiny spores. When the spores are ripe, they shoot out of their containers and fall to the ground or are carried away by the wind.

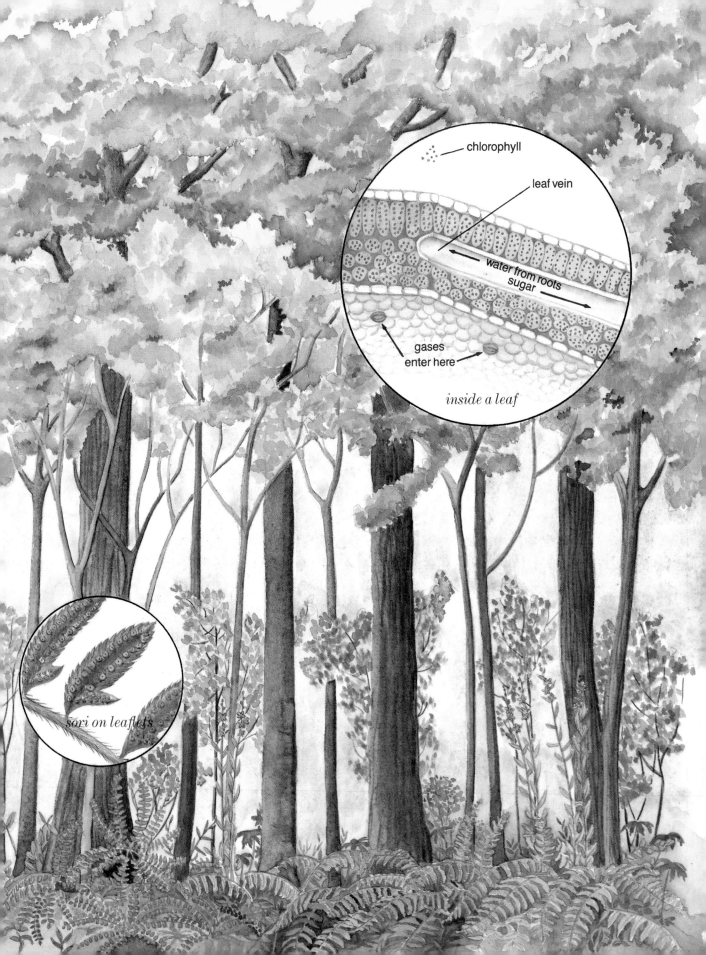

chlorophyll

leaf vein

water from roots
sugar

gases
enter here

inside a leaf

sori on leaflets

FALL—MAMMALS

As the days become shorter again, the bodies of forest mammals start to change. Many of them lose their summer fur. The old hair falls out, and a thicker new coat starts growing in. Some animals, including the ones that hibernate, eat much more at this time of year and build up layers of fat on their bodies. The fat will give warmth and nourishment during the winter. The fall is a busy time for the small mammals that will be active all winter. They scamper through the woods, carrying food to storage places. When winter's snow and ice cover the forest, the food in these hiding places will keep them alive.

During the weeks when they are shedding their summer fur, WEASELS have a patchy look. The new hair growing in is lighter in color than the old summer hair. In the north the new coat will be completely white except for black on the tip of the tail. Weasels in white coats are called *ermines*. Farther south the winter fur is just a lighter brown than the summer coat.

In the fall RACCOONS eat great amounts of food and get very fat. They do not hibernate over the winter, but when cold weather comes, they often stay in their dens for many days at a time. By spring they may weigh only half as much as they did in the fall.

CHIPMUNKS stuff seeds and nuts into little pockets on each side of their mouths. When their cheek pouches are full, they rush off to hide the food in underground nests, in other holes, and under fallen leaves.

SQUIRRELS are busy cutting hickory nuts from the trees and collecting piles of acorns. When they need food in winter, the squirrels will find some of the nuts they have buried by smelling for them along the ground.

FALL — BIRDS

By late summer the birds that hatched this year have flown off to lead independent lives. After the work of raising the young is over for the year, adult birds begin to molt. During these weeks the old, worn feathers drop out one by one, and new ones grow in. This is a dangerous time: The birds cannot fly as well without full sets of wing feathers, and enemies can catch them more easily. It is a period of quiet and secrecy, when most birds stay hidden in the leafy growth of the forest. After the new feathers have grown in, the birds are ready to travel. About three-fourths of the species that nest in these forests will fly south for the winter. Migrating birds from other nesting places also flock to the woodlands at this time. They stop to rest and feed before going on. The great movement of birds ends in late fall after the first killing frosts.

During the molt a bird's feathers fall out according to a regular pattern, which is the same for every bird of that particular kind. Among the small forest birds, the usual pattern is for the long wing feathers to drop in order, starting with feather number one, followed by number two, and so on. When a feather drops, a new one starts growing. Feathers are lost slowly, so the bird is still able to fly during the whole molting period.

Some birds change colors with the fall molt. Male SCARLET TANAGERS have bodies covered with flame red feathers in spring and summer. Dull yellow-green feathers grow in to take their place in fall and winter. During the molt he shows a mixture of green and red patches over his body. Before next spring, the body feathers will fall out again, and bright red ones will grow in.

Adult birds become thinner during the summer because of the energy they use while raising their young. Growing a new set of feathers can also cause loss of weight. After the molt birds eat more food than at other times of the year, and their bodies return to normal weight. The WOOD THRUSH and other birds that fly south eat even more at this time and store the extra food as fat. For them it is fuel for the long journey.

wing feathers

1 2 3 4 5 6 7 8 9

FALL—REPTILES AND AMPHIBIANS

Most reptiles and amphibians begin to move toward their hibernating places as soon as the days and nights start to cool. Tree frogs dig down into rotting tree trunks even in early fall. Snakes begin to gather near their wintering spots. These animals may not go into hibernation for a few more weeks. On warm afternoons they still come out to lie in sunny spots and soak up a little more body heat. But then, as temperatures drop, they disappear silently, one by one slipping into their winter hiding places.

GRAY TREE FROGS have been up in the branches all summer. Jumping from twig to twig, they catch their insect food in midair. Like salamanders, toads, and other frogs, each has inside it an organ called the *fat body* that stores up fat during the summer. By fall, when the animals begin to head for hibernating places, their fat bodies are filled. The fat body supplies nourishment during the winter months.

In cool fall weather BOX TURTLES wander around slowly at all hours, eating every kind of plant and small animal: berries, moss, seeds, mushrooms, and insects, worms, and snails. Sometimes they eat so much that the upper and lower shells of the "box" no longer close tightly.

RED-BACKED SALAMANDERS live their whole lives on the forest floor, hiding in the day and hunting by night. These amphibians mate in the fall, before going underground to hibernate. The female will lay her eggs next summer, in a hole or under a rotting log.

GARTER SNAKES have the longest active season of all eastern snakes. They are the last to go into hibernation, just as they are the first to come out in spring.

FALL—INSECTS

An army of small animals feeds upon dead materials on the forest floor. At this season plants are shedding leaves and nuts. Fallen branches and tree trunks, dead animals, and animal droppings add to the layer on the ground. Insects are part of the cleanup crew. Bit by bit, they tear and chew at the dead matter. In time the layer of waste will be gone, and the chemicals in the dead materials will go back into the soil.

acorn weevil

CARRION BEETLES eat dead animals. Because their bodies are very flat, the beetles can wedge themselves into small openings.

Many acorns on the ground have small, round holes made by ACORN WEEVILS. The females lay eggs inside young acorns while they are still growing on the tree. The larvae hatch and feed on the acorns. After the acorns have fallen, the larvae cut holes and crawl into the soil to spend the winter.

TERMITES are small insects that live in large colonies. The chewing of many worker termites can turn a log into a sponge.

HORNTAILS cut into dead or dying wood in the summertime to lay their eggs. After they have hatched, the larvae live in the wood for a year or more. They dig round tunnels, about the size of a pencil, through the wood.

Small, wingless BRISTLETAILS feed on fallen leaves. They eat the soft parts, leaving only the skeletons of stems and veins.

bristletail

FALL—PLANTS

Shorter days and cool weather signal the end of the green season. The plants have provided for the future by storing up food in their underground parts and in the seeds that hold the promise of new plant life. Now the food factories in the cells of the green leaves shut down. But the leaves cling to the trees for another few weeks. Before they slip to the ground, they brighten the fall woods with a final blaze of color.

Layers of special cells have already formed at the place where a tree leaf is attached to its twig. In the fall these layers grow stiff and block the flow of water coming in from the roots. Without water the chlorophyll in the leaves dies. Now the other colors in the leaves are no longer covered up by the green chlorophyll. Leaves of the SUGAR MAPLE turn red and yellow. Other fall leaves are brown or orange, depending upon the chemical mixture in that particular kind of tree.

Soon tons of dead plant parts shower down on the forest floor: fallen leaves, fruits, seeds, and broken twigs and branches. If they piled up each year, the thick layer would smother all the small plants. Air and sun could not reach the ground, and none of the chemicals in the dead plant parts could be used again by living plants. MUSHROOMS are plants that do not make food for themselves but "feed" on other plants. Mushrooms help to break down the dead layer into bits that will finally become a part of the forest soil.

Ripe nuts fall from the WALNUT trees, and ACORNS rain down from the oaks. Many of the bushes and the low plants of the forest floor also hold bright fruits. Most of this food will be gathered up by the forest animals. Some of the fruits that the animals miss and some of the seeds buried by them will put down roots in some future spring and start new plants.

GLOSSARY

Amphibian. A cold-blooded animal born from an egg that has no shell. All amphibians have toes without claws and most have skin without scales. Many amphibians spend their early life in water and then live on land as adults. Frogs, toads, and salamanders are amphibians.

Bulb. An underground plant part that stores food. Bulbs are short and round and made up of layers of tight scales. An onion is a bulb.

Cambium. A layer inside some plants. Cambium produces the new growth that causes the stems of the plants to become thicker as they grow older.

Cell. One of the tiny building blocks that make up all plant and animal bodies. Most cells are so small that they can be seen only through a microscope.

Chlorophyll. The green matter that gives most plants their color.

Corm. An underground plant part that stores food. Unlike bulbs, the short, thick corms are solid and have only a few scales.

*Larva (*plural: *larvae).* A stage in the life of some insects, coming after they hatch from the egg and before they change to pupae.

Nymph. A stage in the life of some insects, coming after they hatch from the egg and before they change to adults. Insects that become nymphs do not pass through the stages of larva and pupa.

Phloem. The layer in a plant stem that is just outside the cambium. Food moves to all parts of the plant through the phloem.

*Pupa (*plural: *pupae).* A resting period in the life of some insects, coming between the larva stage and the adult. As a pupa, some insects are enclosed in a covering that protects them.

Reptile. A cold-blooded animal with scales on its skin and claws on its toes. Most hatch from eggs that have tough shells, but the young of some reptiles are born alive. Turtles, lizards, and snakes are reptiles.

Rhizome. An underground plant part that stores food. Rhizomes grow level with the surface of the ground and may be quite long.

Sapwood. The layer in a plant stem that is just inside the cambium. Water and dissolved chemicals move up to the leaves through the sapwood.

Tuber. An underground plant part that stores food. Tubers are short and thick and often grow at the ends of rhizomes. A potato is a tuber.

INDEX

Italics indicate illustrations.

Shelf List

3 4598 00010456 5

J 574.5-LER   A forest year

Lerner, Carol

DATE DUE

OCT 1 _ 1996	WITHDRAWN		
EC 1 8 1996			
MAR 1 8 1997			
APR 3 0 1997			
MAY 1 9 1997			
OCT 2 6 2000			
JUN 1 3 2001			
OCT 9 2001			
MAR 2 2 2009			
SEP 1 7 2003			
NOV 1 6 2010			
JUN 3 2011			

GAYLORD   PRINTED IN U.S.A.

Pease Public Library
Plymouth, NH 03264-1414